CW01095551

THE OFFICIAL
wolves
ANNUAL 2011

Written by Paul Berry

Designed by Brian Thomson

A Grange Publication

© 2010. Published by Grange Communications Ltd., Edinburgh under licence from Wolverhampton Wanderers Football Club.

Printed in the EU.

Photography © AMA Sports Photo Agency

ISBN: 978-1-907104-79-4

£7.99

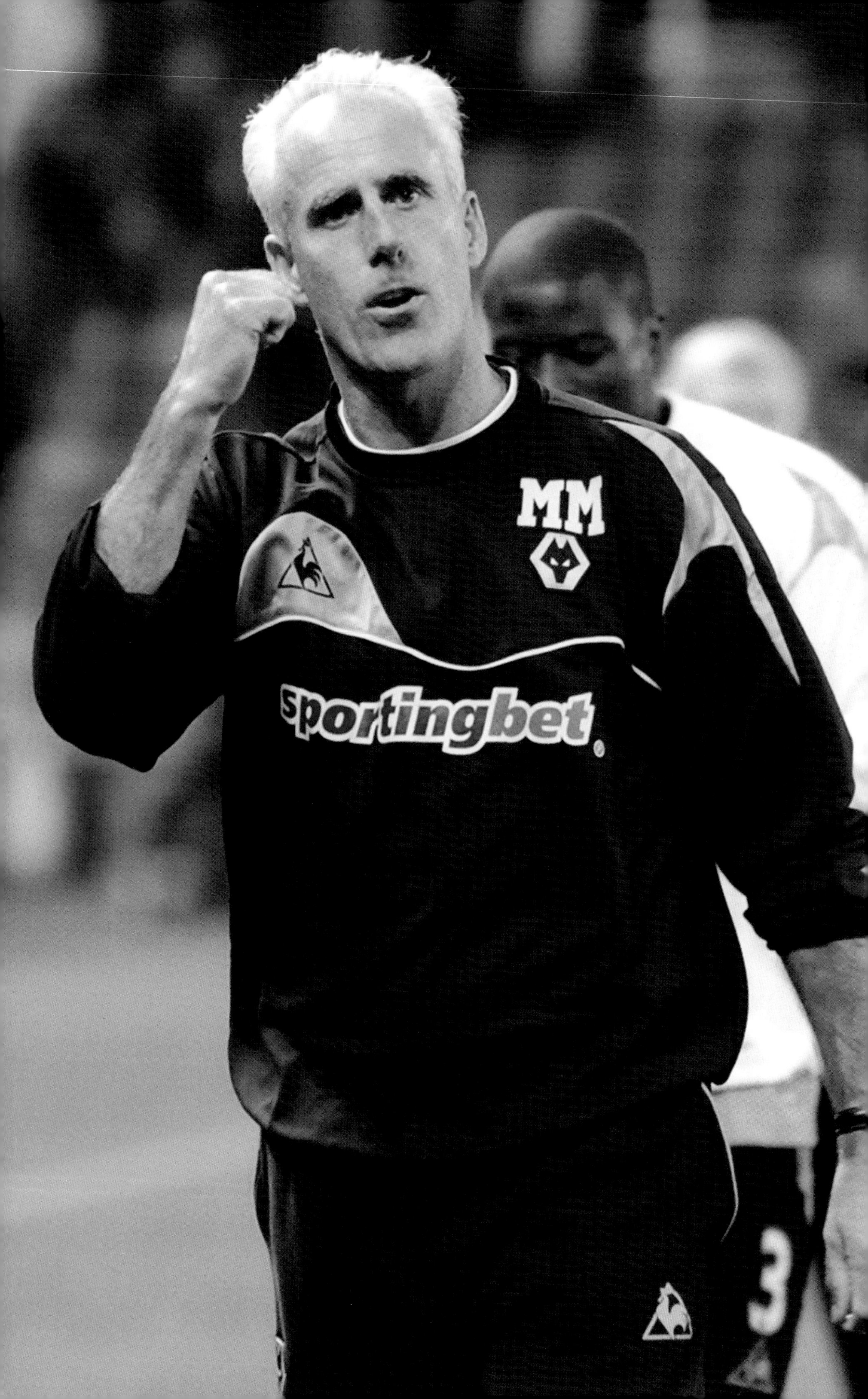
MM
sportingbet

CONTENTS

MICK McCARTHY
BOSS'S PRIDE

It is now over 18 years since Mick McCarthy first entered the managerial hotseat as player-boss at Millwall.

Pretty much a generation!

And the Wolves manager will readily admit it never gets any easier. McCarthy was still a player in the early stages of his career with hometown club Barnsley the last time Wolves survived a season in the top flight when John Barnwell was boss in the 1980/81 campaign.

But he helped mastermind a repeat performance last season with a team which got better and better and lost just two of the final 11 games to finish 15th and eventually survive with two matches to spare.

He was then delighted to be able to add to that by bringing in players over the summer who already had Barclays Premier League experience under their belt.

"That theory of mine – that the players would pick up experience - was proved by the fact that the longer the season went on the better they got," said McCarthy.

"We didn't start brilliantly – we did alright– but we grew into it and only lost two in 10 at the end of the season.

"That proves they improved and got better.

"If you get better over three quarters of a season they've all improved and then bringing in players with that Premier League experience already has got to be good."

It is a sign of McCarthy's managerial abilities that in those 18 years in the dugout he has only occupied four different positions.

Millwall, the Republic of Ireland, Sunderland and now Wolves. And with only about seven months spent away from the game.

That experience and know-how means he certainly wasn't getting carried away by last season's survival which was clinched as Burnley lost to Liverpool on a Spring Sunday afternoon when McCarthy was out riding his bike.

He knew heading into the current campaign that there was another massive test in store.

"It may be less arduous because we have stayed in the league but there will still be the 'second season syndrome' that people talk about and thinking it was a fluke," he explained.

"If we do that we can build on it."

If Wolves are to survive again this season it will once again also need the excellent support of the club's fans.

The transformation of Wolves since McCarthy's arrival in the summer of 2006 has been achieved amid an ethos of young and talented players who have certainly given everything they have for the club's fanbase.

"I think our fans were terrific last season – they supported us and were fantastic," said the boss.

"I think they reacted like their team was the underdog last season – they got behind us and it was great.

"And absolutely - the fans need to be the same again this season.

"They need to have that 'chip on the shoulder' mentality of 'us against everyone else'.

"It doesn't need to be an attitude of the world is against us but when you're playing, that kind of approach does create a good team spirit and ethic."

All music to the ears of a manager still relishing each and every day of life in the Wolves' hotseat.

"If we could survive again then it would be another season in the Premier League towards building the club back to 'something like'."

"Stoke have done it – surviving two seasons and getting better – and other teams have done it.

"I'll just follow the process of having the players in and working with them with TC (Terry Connor) and the staff and getting the best out of them.

"We're not on parity and are bucking the trend against the big fellows who all think they should turn up and slap us.

"But we managed to dent their expectations on a couple of occasions last season.

"We've done it once and have now got to work just as hard as last season - and probably harder - to stay in it again.

GREAT SCOT!
FLETCH CHECKS IN

It's fair to say that most transfer targets for a club are watched time and time again by the manager and scouting staff before a decision is made on whether to sign them.

But not many have to play in front of the whole team!

That's what happened with striker Steven Fletcher two years ago, when turning out for Hibernian in a glamorous pre-season friendly with Barcelona at Murrayfield.

Mick McCarthy took his entire coaching and playing staff to the game as a bit of a break from training during Wolves' pre-season tour of Scotland.

Barca put on a masterclass in pass-and-move football in comfortably seeing off Hibs 6-0, and while Fletcher the player was already catching the eye of the Wolves manager, he wasn't expecting much from him that evening!

"Nobody really shone in that game I can assure you of that," said Mick.

"Hibernian got 'mullered' on that night!

"Steven is a player who had been on the radar of Taff (head of European scouting Ian Evans) and (Chief Scout) Dave Bowman for a long time and they persuaded me to take a look at him.

"I did that, but we'd made all our signings last season by the time he went to Burnley.

"I'm just delighted we managed to get him this summer and he was our primary target for the striker's position.

"He's impressed me every time I've seen him and he had a great first season in the Premier League.

"His all-round ability is excellent - he's a worker who grafts and makes the ball stick and will fit in with us and what I expect from players."

Fletcher was also delighted to have checked in at Wolves, where he became the club's joint record signing alongside fellow frontman Kevin Doyle.

"I always wanted to play in the Premier League when I was up the road in Scotland," he said. "It's great that I've got another chance to do that with Wolves. "Last season with Burnley brought on my game a lot as it would do playing against the quality of opposition in the Premier League.

"Moving to Wolves I want to try and bring that here and improve again - I want to come here and score goals and hopefully bring that to the team.

Changing sides – in action for Burnley against Richard Stearman

It's going to get Messi against Barcelona's Lionel

Winning the header against Daniel Alves

And Berra is pleased to now be able to count Fletcher as a friend rather than foe.

"Fletch is a very good player," he says.

"I've played against him many a time in big derby games and we've have a few good battles along the way!

"He's a good lad and will be a good addition to the squad and fits in to what the gaffer always looks for.

"When we were up there and there was a lot of press about the younger boys, it was always Fletch and myself who were mentioned and we got our moves here within a few months of each other.

"Hopefully we've both shown we can play well in the Premier League and can continue to improve as we carry on playing here."

"Hopefully we can have another good season just like Wolves did last year.

"I think Wolves are moving in the right direction and pushing forward and hopefully we can do the same again next season and stay in the Premier League and even maybe finish higher up the table."

Well known to the manager and indeed to most of his team-mates there was one face in the Molineux dressing room who Fletcher had already played alongside before.

Fellow Scot Christophe Berra.

While they've been on the same side of the fence on international duty they also enjoyed a few ding-dongs on opposite teams when involved in Edinburgh derbies with Hearts and Hibernian.

Above: Welcome to Wolves! Mick greets Steven Fletcher.

Main Pic, Opposite Page: Flying the flag, Fletcher gets settled in.

SEASON REVIEW 2009/10

AUGUST

There was much optimism around Molineux for the first game of the season back on August 15, 2009.

A successful pre-season tour of Australia and the usual busy friendly programme prepared Wolves well for their return to the Barclays Premier League and a date with West Ham.

But on a sunny afternoon – isn't that always the case on the opening day? – the harsh realities of top flight football hit home as despite long periods of pressure Wolves fell victim to the sucker punches of a goal in each half from Mark Noble and Matthew Upson.

Mick McCarthy's team however are not known for raising the white flag, and despite heading to a buoyant Wigan team three days later shorn of injured pair Sylvan Ebanks-Blake and Kevin Foley, it was to prove an historic night.

> *"I think we've shown the rest of the Premier League that we can perform at this level and we want to stay here."*
>
> *Richard Stearman*

Andy Keogh's early header proved the only goal of the game at the JJB Stadium, earning Wolves their first away win in the top flight for 25 years.

A second half improvement at moneybags Manchester City wasn't enough to avoid a 1-0 defeat, and after edging out Swindon on penalties in the Carling Cup the month was completed with the visit of Hull.

In the sort of game in which Wolves would be hoping to post positive results, it needed a fine finish from Richard Stearman to grab his team a draw but four points from the first four fixtures laid some decent foundations for the rest of the campaign.

Left: Stephen Ward and goalscorer Andy Keogh celebrate at Wigan.
Top right: Richard Stearman fires home against Hull.

SEPTEMBER

The month began with a double-header of international fixtures, with Wolves summer signing Nenad Milijaš scoring from the penalty spot for Serbia against France to put his team on the brink of World Cup qualification.

Not so good news however for Wolves, as one of their few below-par displays of the season resulted in a 3-1 defeat at Blackburn, a late debut goal from substitute Stefan Maierhofer offering little consolation.

Again though the team bounced straight back, a first Wolves goal for record signing Kevin Doyle and excellent finish from Dave Edwards paving the way for a 2-1 home win against Fulham that lifted the club to the dizzy heights of 12th in the table.

"It's the sort of evening where we feel like we've had our head rubbed and our belly tickled and sent off down the road with a 'Thanks for coming'. And I don't like that."

**Mick McCarthy,
post-Manchester United**

Next up attention switched to the Carling Cup, and despite a performance packed with promise, Wolves went down 1-0 to ten-man Manchester United thanks to a second half goal from Danny Welbeck.

The final weekend of the month proved a real bitter-sweet affair.

Two goals down to Sunderland at the Stadium of Light, Wolves hit back to level matters before conceding three late goals to leave the Wearsiders celebrating a hugely flattering 5-2 victory.

Above: A new hero! Kevin Doyle celebrates his first Wolves goal.
Top right: Mick McCarthy shares a joke with Steve Bruce on his latest return to Sunderland.

OCTOBER

October got off to the worst possible start as Wolves became the first team to lose against Portsmouth in the season.

Hassan Yebda's first half header proved the only goal of the game but Wolves could have been awarded a lifeline only for referee Howard Webb to miss a blatant second half handball from Pompey defender Marc Wilson which should have resulted in a penalty.

"The fans here have been great to me even when I wasn't playing. They seem like the best fans in the country and I can only thank them for their support."
Ronald Zubar

Another international break meant a fortnight of waiting to put things right, but Wolves almost did to spectacular effect when another Kevin Doyle goal took them within minutes of a famous win at Everton.

Toffees' winger Dimitar Bilyaetdinov – Billy to his mates – equalised two minutes from the end after which there was still time for Stefan Maierhofer to be sent off.

The following weekend it was Wolves grateful for a late goal when Sylvan Ebanks-Blake's penalty cancelled out Gabby Agbonlahor's finish for Aston Villa as the spoils were shared in the Midlands derby.

A third successive hard-earned point followed, this time at the Britannia Stadium, with a 2-0 half time deficit at Stoke snuffed out by a brace from the evergreen Jody Craddock.

Top Right: Ronald Zubar made his first league start at Goodison Park.
Above: Sylvan Ebanks-Blake after netting from the spot against Villa.

NOVEMBER

Wolves hit the beach at the start of November, Curracloe Beach in Wexford for a light training session ahead of a friendly with Kevin Doyle's former club as part of the deal which took him to Molineux.

Doyle was certainly a popular attraction during the brief trip to Ireland as goals from Stefan Maierhofer and Andy Keogh earned Wolves a 2-1 friendly win.

Back to business in the league and it was the might of Arsenal who visited Molineux in the club's Help For Heroes game, and departed with a 4-1 win.

It didn't get any easier seven days later at Stamford Bridge, as another of the Premier League's harshest assignments saw Wolves comfortably despatched 4-0 by Chelsea.

The perhaps unsurprising double defeats at the hands of two of the 'Big Four' left Wolves entrenched in the relegation zone, and things were to get worse before they got better.

"I've said to the lads that we're in a relegation dogfight and there's no point making any bones about it."

Mick McCarthy, post-Chelsea

A high noon derby showdown with Birmingham saw Wolves produce one of their worst displays of the season and defeat to Lee Bowyer's early chip left Mick McCarthy's men four points adrift of safety by the end of the month.

Top Right: Irish eyes are smiling as Andy Keogh and Kevin Doyle return 'home'.
Left: Tanks a lot! Over £24,000 was raised for Armed Forces charities after the 'Help For Heroes' game with Arsenal.

> "My only concern is Wolves, the people at this club and the supporters. Everyone else I don't give two hoots about."
>
> **Mick McCarthy,**
> **post-Manchester United**

DECEMBER

The pressure was on as Wolves headed into a home game with Bolton without a win in eight games and sitting 19th in the table.

But once again the team delivered, Jody Craddock scoring Wolves' fourth goal in a row early on and Nenad Milijaš adding a second half piledriver in the 2-1 win.

Even better however was to follow as Wolves travelled to a Tottenham team chasing Champions League qualification and buoyant after sticking nine goals past Wigan in their previous home game.

Wolves were simply magnificent at White Hart Lane, producing another early goal through Kevin Doyle and then defending superbly to limit an excellent Spurs side to few clear-cut chances.

After the lung-bursting exertions of that game, Mick McCarthy chose to make ten changes for the midweek encounter at Manchester United, a decision that earned one or two column inches in the press afterwards!

But while Wolves lost 3-0, they were right in the game for the first half an hour and could have gone in front through George Friend.

A return to winning ways quickly followed as goals from Milijaš and Doyle saw off Burnley at Molineux, and Wolves were also troubling Liverpool at Anfield on Boxing Day until Stephen Ward's controversial sending-off shortly after half time.

Liverpool then struck twice, but only after Wolves had been reduced in numbers, and while the year finished with a 3-0 home defeat to Manchester City, a league placing of 15th left the club in a decent position going into 2010.

This Page
Top: Delight for boss Mick McCarthy at White Hart Lane.
Right: Nenad Milijaš found his scoring touch in December.

Opposite Page
Top: Adlene Guedioura and Geoffrey Mujangi Bia arrived from RSC Charleroi.
Bottom: Pick that one out! Ronald Zubar nets against Crystal Palace.

JANUARY

Wolves kicked off the New Year with an FA Cup trip to Tranmere on a frozen Sunday evening, a goal from Matt Jarvis securing a hard-fought passage into the fourth round.

The postponement of the following league game at West Ham – more on that later! – meant Wolves were next in action at home to Wigan, a disappointing afternoon where, after Richard Stearman's sending-off, they succumbed to two second half goals.

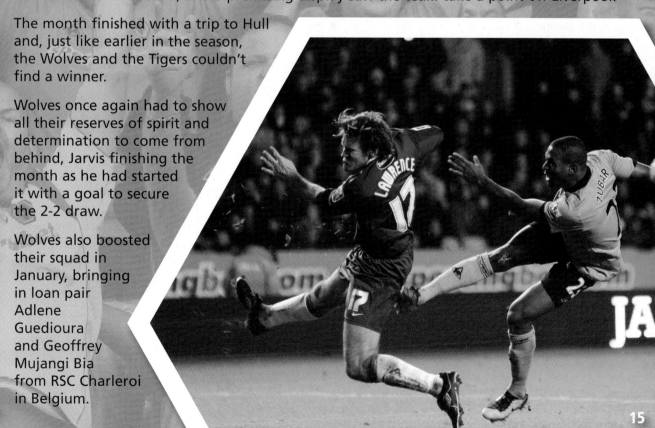

Switching back to the FA Cup, it needed a late Ronald Zubar thunderbolt, the Frenchman's first goal for the club, to equalise late on at home to Crystal Palace to secure a replay after David Jones's first of the season provided an initial equaliser.

And then, ahead of a Tuesday night meeting with Liverpool at Molineux, boss Mick McCarthy made a decision which was to prove key to Wolves' prospects of survival.

"I've watched the Premier League so many times on television from when I was very young and it is a dream come true to be here playing in it now."
Adlene Guedioura

A regular exponent of 4-4-2 formation, the boss opted to go 4-3-3- or 4-5-1 to try and make Wolves more solid, and a promising display saw the team take a point off Liverpool.

The month finished with a trip to Hull and, just like earlier in the season, the Wolves and the Tigers couldn't find a winner.

Wolves once again had to show all their reserves of spirit and determination to come from behind, Jarvis finishing the month as he had started it with a goal to secure the 2-2 draw.

Wolves also boosted their squad in January, bringing in loan pair Adlene Guedioura and Geoffrey Mujangi Bia from RSC Charleroi in Belgium.

FEBRUARY

February began in disappointing fashion with two away defeats, albeit in vastly different circumstances.

The FA Cup fourth round replay at Crystal Palace witnessed one of Wolves' poorer displays of the season with an astonishing seven-minute hat trick from irregular scorer Ian Butterfield helping the Eagles soar to a 3-1 victory.

"There were 18 passes and it was finished off really well – had it been Arsenal or Chelsea scoring it I think people would be raving about it and it would keep being shown from start to finish."

Karl Henry

The following – and much shorter – trip down the road to St Andrew's produced a far better performance and with ten minutes to go Wolves were on the verge of an impressive away success thanks to another Kevin Doyle goal.

But heartache was to follow courtesy of familiar nemesis Kevin Phillips, who came off the bench to grab two late goals and once again push Wolves back into the relegation zone.

Again though they responded, securing an excellent midweek win over Tottenham which ensured a first league double of the season.

The excellence of the result was matched by the excellence of the goal, David Jones finishing off an 18-pass move which proved an example of possession football at its best.

It was a timely result and a crucial one, because next up Chelsea departed Molineux with the points courtesy of a 2-0 win despite a promising Wolves performance.

And a 1-0 defeat at fellow battlers Bolton on the final weekend of the month saw luck desert a Wolves side who twice shot against the inside of the post in the second half.

Above: Karl Henry battling with Michael Ballack against Chelsea.
Right: David Jones celebrates the excellent team goal against Tottenham.

MARCH

Manchester United were the first visitors to Molineux in March for a Saturday evening kick off.

And Wolves produced another accomplished team performance to stay with United all the way up until Paul Scholes notched a clinical 73rd-minute goal.

Even then there was chance for Wolves to hit back, Sam Vokes left distraught after shooting over the bar a minute into injury time.

The result left Wolves just outside the relegation zone ahead of a crucial hat-trick of claret and blue awaydays at Burnley, Aston Villa and West Ham.

"The team is gelling and we've been solid – we're taking our chances when they come along and hopefully we can keep improving."
Kevin Doyle

The first two went swimmingly, an excellent battling win at Turf Moor followed by the equally welcome acquisition of a point at Villa Park as the teams shared four goals.

But it was in the performance at Upton Park on March 23rd that Wolves took a major stride towards survival.

Separated by just a point prior to the game, it was Mick McCarthy's side which produced a blistering display capped by goals from Kevin Doyle, Ronald Zubar and Matt Jarvis.

The 3-1 victory couldn't have come at a better time and remember – this was the fixture initially postponed in January and then re-scheduled a second time due to the Crystal Palace cup replay.

Wolves rounded off March by adding another vital point to the tally, grinding out a goalless draw at home to an Everton team very much in form.

Top: Matt Jarvis completes Wolves' scoring on a special night at Upton Park.
Right: Christophe Berra goes toe-to-toe with Villa striker Emile Heskey.

April began with a trip to Arsenal marking Wolves' first ever fixture at the Emirates Stadium.

And it could have been a near-perfect first visit as Wolves blunted the Gunners for long periods up until a hugely controversial decision when referee Andre Marriner sent Karl Henry off following a challenge on Tomas Rosicky.

That dismissal came in the 65th minute, but Wolves still held Arsenal at bay until the fourth minute of injury time when Nicolas Bentdner agonisingly headed home to cruelly leave the Molineux Men empty-handed.

A Sunday lunchtime date with Stoke followed, the first of three games in which Wolves were unjustly without their suspended skipper Henry.

Despite his absence, and a relative torrent of long throws from Rory Delap, Wolves held firm to secure a goalless draw which they then followed up with another against Fulham at Craven Cottage.

That left a home game with Blackburn with which to complete the month, at which Wolves knew three points would pretty well secure survival.

As it was they gleaned one, thanks to a header from Sylvan Ebanks-Blake a couple of minutes after coming off the bench in the game's latter stages.

Yet results elsewhere left Wolves on the brink of clinching Barclays Premier League status, a feat which was duly achieved when Burnley were beaten by Liverpool 24 hours later.

"I went out for a bike ride so didn't follow any of the (Burnley) game. I came back and had a shower and when I came downstairs Fiona (Mick's wife) told me it was 2-0 to Liverpool. Happy days!"
Mick McCarthy

Top: The agony – heartache as Karl Henry is dismissed at the Emirates.
Right: The ecstasy – fans celebrate Sylvan Ebanks-Blake's equaliser against Blackburn.

MAY

With the season's main objective – survival – safely assured, it was perhaps always going to be difficult to maintain the same level of intensity which had brought Wolves the prospect of successive top flight seasons for the first time in almost 30 years.

Under that background they made the long trip to Fratton Park for the season's final away game against a Portsmouth side which while already relegated themselves, were in party atmosphere ahead of their appearance in the FA Cup Final.

And so it was that with Wolves ever so slightly taking their foot off the pedal, Pompey ran out 3-1 winners.

But chastened by that slight drop in standards, Wolves were keen to go out on a high in front of their own fans on the final day of the season against Sunderland.

"As I said on the pitch after the game, I'm delighted with the way the players have gone about their business this season and am very proud of them. It's a great achievement."
Mick McCarthy

A Kevin Doyle penalty, his ninth goal of the season, cancelled out Kenwyne Jones' opener and Adlene Guedioura's first for Wolves in the second period secured the win that produced a neat final tally of 38 points from 38 games and a final and respectable position of 15th.

With Doyle having won the Players' Player of the Year award, Craddock was presented with the Supporters' trophy and the players enjoyed a well-received lap of honour around Molineux to reflect on a job very well done.

*Top: Coolness personified, Kevin Doyle converts from the spot against Sunderland.
Right: Chairman Steve Morgan reflects on an excellent Wolves season.*

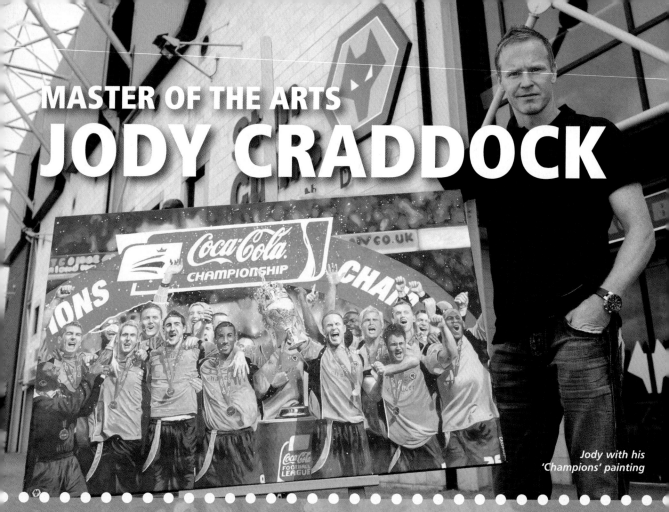

MASTER OF THE ARTS
JODY CRADDOCK

Jody with his 'Champions' painting

Like a fine wine, Jody Craddock just seems to have got better and better with age.

So much so that last season he not only started almost all of Wolves' fixtures in the Barclays Premier League, he ended up walking away with the Supporters' Player of the Year award at the end of it.

Not to mention a new contract which took his time at Molineux into an eighth year, no small feat for any player at any club in the modern era.

Craddock, who also made his 500th league appearance during the 2009/10 season, is also a hugely popular figure off the field as well as on it.

One of those who can be relied on by his manager and team-mates as a true professional.

A devoted family man to wife Shelley and three sons Joseph, Luke and Toby, there is of course another major string to Craddock's bow – his hobby of art.

The word hobby actually does it a great disservice as the footballer-turned-artist was actually an artist before he was a footballer – and is also extremely good!

The Wolves Annual **(WA)** caught up with the defender to find out more...

Above: That's my boy! Jody's son Joseph immortalised on canvas
For more of Jody's paintings and prints visit
www.craddock-art.com and www.art-affect.com

WA: Hi Jody. When was it that you first started doing a bit of art?

JC: I started at school by doing A-level in Art. It went a bit quiet after that when I became a footballer. But when I went to Sunderland I had a bit more money and was able to buy some oils. Before I'd done a bit of sketching and watercolours but the more oil painting I did the better I got.

WA: Did art come naturally to you?

JC: It does run in the family a little bit as my Dad can draw and my Great Grandad was very good as well. That's probably helped but I've also got an eye for art and an eye for a picture. But I think anyone can draw or paint if they practise enough, and that's what I've done really. The more I did the better I got although going from drawing pictures and paintings to actually selling them was quite a step!

WA: Do you focus on any particular theme for your art?

JC: I like to do a variety of different subjects from contemporary portraitures to landscapes and wildlife. I don't want to be pigeon holed and will always paint what feels right to me. It's not my main job but I know a lot of painters will just stick to one style whereas I like the variety so I can develop my skills.

WA: Have you had your work exhibited?

JC: I did an exhibition up in Sunderland just as I was leaving and did one earlier this year at the NEC's Spring Fair in Birmingham which was good. I've had another piece of work in an exhibition at the Public in Walsall.

WA: Have you had much feedback from the players?

JC: It's a great job being a footballer but doing the painting as well means there are always footballers who want pictures of themselves! Maybe it's scoring a goal or celebrating. I've always had a fair bit of interest since Sunderland and have done a lot of different paintings here as well. I did a play-off picture for Sir Jack (Hayward) when I first came to the club, I did the 'Champions' one when we lifted the Championship trophy and have done one of the huddle as well. I've also done numerous paintings for the lads individually and Kights and Lumes both had one done.

WA: When do you find time to work on your art?

JC: I tend to do my painting in the evenings. With the football and having three kids it's the only real chance I get! I suppose it has got more serious than just a hobby but it's still very relaxing and a good way to unwind. I've also branched out more into the print side of things as well which people can see from the website. While I'm in my studio at home I can just forget all about football and concentrate on the painting. After all, I'm a man, I can't think about two things at once! Football and painting? No chance! It's just a good release from the everyday job!

WA: How long does it take to work on a painting from start to finish?

JC: I do my paintings in stages, from the back forwards. You do need patience but I'm actually not the most patient when it comes to it. Some painters spend hours and hours on their work and I've seen one in Cornwall who spends 400 hours on each painting! I was like: Wow! I use oils and work quite quickly and my paintings usually take about 15 hours. It might sound a lot to people but to a painter that's probably not too long at all.
I am quite impatient but oils suit my style which mean I can work quite quickly.

WA: Do they cause much discussion among the players?

JC: There's always banter in the dressing room but not too much about my paintings to be fair. If I'd done them and they were rubbish I'd probably be getting some right old stick! The players are good critics. If they buy one and like it then they tell their mates who want one which is great.

Above: The Wolves huddle

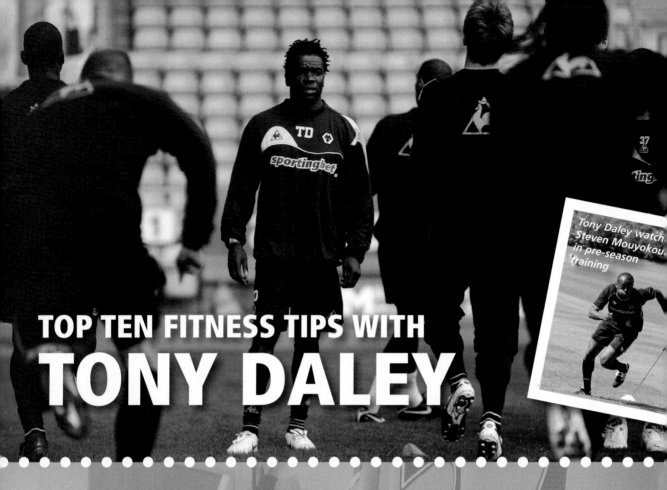

TOP TEN FITNESS TIPS WITH
TONY DALEY

Tony Daley watch Steven Mouyokou in pre-season training

Staying fit and healthy is a crucial part of any footballer's make-up, and at Wolves, that responsibility falls to Fitness and Conditioning Coach Tony Daley. But fitness is an area which extends to all walks of life, not just sport. Here Dales gives some top tips for anyone wishing to keep themselves in good shape.

Christophe Berra leads the fitness knees-up!

1 Think of your body as a top of the range sports car. It is far more complex than any sports car and yet we treat our cars far better than we treat ourselves in a lot of cases. We get our cars serviced to make them run better and replace worn out parts and make sure they run properly by putting in the best oil and hold the road with the best tyres. How do we treat our bodies? We expect them to run really well even though we work them hard and do not refuel them correctly and when we get pain from strains caused by slipping because we are wearing the wrong footwear we keep on training until the muscle pulls or in worst cases tears.

2 Ensure you eat well and if you are training try and intake protein every four to five hours to prevent your body taking it from your lean muscle area. Try something like a Multipower fit protein or fitness shake and protein bar.

3 Maintain good fluid intake during the day by drinking two litres of water. This will keep your body hydrated and ensure all the nutrients are passed round as quick as possible. During training maintain energy by drinking an energy drink or for weight loss L-carnitine which turns fat to energy if combined with exercise.

Tony and other backroom staff look on as Matt Jarvis undergoes a VO2 Max Test

7 Recover properly by taking the correct nutrition to replace the protein and carbohydrates you have burned during exercise. This will ensure that the muscles will repair and grow.

8 Listen to your body. If your car starts making a noise or a warning light comes on you get it fixed to prevent it breaking down. Your body is more complex and the effects of not listening to it could be far worse. It will tell you by giving you a pain warning of various degrees if it has a problem with muscles/joints etc. Don't ignore the pain as this could lead to a more serious injury which could mean a long lay off from training and playing games.

Kevin Foley on the revolutionary Alter-G machine which takes a recovering players' body weight

9 Get the required sleep which helps the body recover and take something like Multipower Formula 80. It contains caseinate whey protein which will digest slowly through the night to ensure your body gets the required amino acids while you are sleeping. It can also be taken at breakfast or lunchtime if you haven't got time to prepare something.

4 Wear the correct clothing and footwear for the conditions. We replace tyres when they are worn to prevent accidents so make sure you wear the correct training shoes or football/ rugby boots to prevent you slipping which can cause muscle strains and pulls and in worst cases tears or ligament injuries.

10 Enjoy your training and set yourself fitness goals and try to be as fit as you can. The top sides in any sport or any athlete regardless of ability all have one thing in common – they work extremely hard at being as fit as they can to achieve their status.

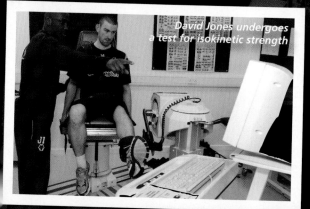

David Jones undergoes a test for isokinetic strength

5 Warm up and stretch correctly before starting your training session and always do your stretches after a session to prevent injury.

6 If you are football training, train with the same intensity as if you're playing a game.

Keeper Carl Ikeme in some Functional Movement Screening fitness work

QUIZ PAGE

SPOT THE FIRST ELEVEN!

FIND THE WOLVES PLAYERS BELOW IN THE WORDSEARCH:

HAHNEMANN

ZUBAR

BERRA

CRADDOCK

ELOKOBI

KIGHTLY

FOLEY

HENRY

JONES

WARD

DOYLE

B	H	A	H	N	E	M	A	N	N
B	E	R	E	J	L	L	D	S	Z
C	N	R	N	L	O	T	O	D	U
K	R	J	R	F	K	N	L	O	B
I	Y	A	P	A	O	W	E	V	A
G	E	R	D	R	B	L	A	S	R
H	L	V	O	D	I	B	E	R	K
T	O	I	Y	G	O	A	T	Y	D
L	P	S	L	F	Z	C	R	O	T
Y	A	L	E	J	U	E	K	A	P

JUMBLED ELEVEN!

REARRANGE THE WORDS BELOW TO DISCOVER THE NAME OF A MEMBER OF WOLVES' MANAGEMENT OR PLAYING STAFF FROM THE 2009/10 SEASON.

THY CRAM KIM CC

DINE LOVEY K

LARK HE RYN

BRAN OR ZUALD

CRY ROTER NON

LAKE BANK VANS BEYLS

SEW RAVE DADD

HE YAWNS SEEN YEN

DATE LONYY

IM A RATS TJV

DOC DOC DAK JYR

KARL HENRY

CELEBRITY WOLVES FAN
SUZI SPEAKS!

It's fair to say that TV personality Suzi Perry has now become one of the most recognisable people on our TV screens. Her CV boasts an extensive and diverse range of broadcasting assignments from the day she first broke into the industry with Sky Sports back in 1997.

She is perhaps most well known for presenting The Gadget Show on Five as well as contributing to all manner of BBC's sports coverage and for the best part of a decade being the face of Moto GP, the premier Motorcycle Racing series. Above all that though, Suzi is fiercely proud not only of her Wolverhampton upbringing but also her passionate support of her favourite football team – Wolves! Having been a keen supporter not only from the stands but also down the years with club events, she is also a patron of leading children's charity Promise Dreams (www.promisedreams.co.uk) alongside Steve Bull and Don Goodman. The Wolves Annual caught up with Suzi, to find out more about her Wolves background!

Q: Hi Suzi. Can you remember when you first became a Wolves fan and how it happened?!

A: I have always been a Wolves fan, I inherited the passion. My grandfather was asked to try out for the team, but his father wouldn't allow him to because he worked in his butchers shop on a Saturday! My father and brother are also keen footie players, my dad used to have his own team and my 'bro' coaches a kids team so I have grown up with the sport and being brought up in Wolverhampton, becoming an old gold and black fan was always on the cards.

Q: Who were your heroes in the early days?

A: I remember loving John Richards, I was a big fan. Then when Emlyn Hughes came to see out the end of his career, I got terribly over-excited when I found out that he was lodging with someone who lived in our road! I made a card in the shape of a Wolf head and took it to him - he was very kind and chatted to me about the club.

Q: Did you used to get to many games as a youngster? Any particular memories/funny stories?!

A: I was involved in a lot of my own activities when I was younger, I played for every team at Smestow School and we had matches on a Saturday. And I also took dance classes, so I didn't get to matches until I was older. I did make it to the training ground a couple of times to collect a few autographs such as Derek Dougan, Willie Carr, 'JR' etc. Now I watch from the directors box so have to mind my p's and q's!

Q: How often do you manage to get to games now amid your busy schedule and how much do you enjoy getting along to Molineux?

A: I love the hallowed ground! Unfortunately it's difficult for me to get to matches now though because I live in the South of France. I probably make five or six a season. I always either watch on TV or listen to the radio though, I can't stand not knowing what's going on and my brother always messages me pics from the ground. He, my nephew and my dad all have season tickets in the Steve Bull stand.

Q: Given that your jobs have seen you travel around the world, how proud are you to say you're from Wolverhampton and support Wolves?

A: I am very proud of my roots and am quite defensive of the town if someone tries to have a pop! I loved growing up in Wolverhampton, my family still live there and I adore coming back. My memories of childhood are mainly good ones! And it will always be my true home.

Q: Do you try and convert other people you work with and celebrities to the cause of Wolves?!!!

A: I think that you have to have a reason to support a team, I am not a fan of people who have tenuous links! So, no, I don't try to convert!

Q: What were your thoughts on last season and survival in the Premier League? Any particular highlights?

A: I thought that the campaign came together towards the end of the season. We only lost two games in the last 10, which is pretty amazing in the Premiership. I felt that Mick was vindicated with his controversial decision to field a certain team against Manchester Utd! And overall, I think that the boys persevered well and played some good football. I felt that the highlight was the improvement of the team, their concentration and discipline which kept them in the right place.

Q: How impressed have you been with the job done by Mick McCarthy? Have you managed to meet him much?

A: I have met Mick, I'm a big fan. I like his no-nonsense attitude. I think he has assembled a good young squad and wish him every success for next season.

Q: How hopeful are you for the club next season and moving forward?

A: Well I think this year was a tough one and this coming season will also be very tricky. And of course we'll have to deal with the 'Baggies' again! But if they can keep their heads and have more self belief, then there is no reason why Wolves can't move up the table. They have the talent and the manager!

Q: Finally, which player or players would you like to invite on The Gadget Show and why?

A: Wolves are a team. Jody Craddock and Kevin Doyle may have been seen as the star players last season, but I think their strength is playing as a team. So I would like them all to come on the show - we could test goal-line technology!

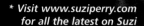

* Visit www.suziperry.com for all the latest on Suzi

27

THE WOLVES PLAYERS, AS YOU'VE NEVER SEEN THEM BEFORE!

Towards the end of last season, Wolves staged their first ever Fashion Show involving the players, in conjunction with top Birmingham store Harvey Nichols and in aid of Everyman, the leading charity promoting awareness of testicular and prostate cancer.

A packed Hayward Suite at Molineux then played host to a thoroughly enjoyable, and indeed professional, night with no fewer than 10 Wolves players joining a group of fully fledged female models in putting on a great show.

Over 200 guests turned out for the event, including those among the Wolves squad who weren't involved in the show itself, who offered their own brand of 'support' from the sidelines.

Thousands of points were raised for Everyman, and it's fair to say the players certainly enjoyed their spell in a different sort of limelight.

Some French flair from Ronald Zubar

Mick McCarthy and the team said they'd love to get involved.

Everyman is a charity very close to footballer's hearts and we asked for ten players and within ten minutes we had ten names.

Hat's off to Wolves, they have been a fantastic club to work with.

Kevin Breese (Harvey Nichols)

A stylish scarf for George Elokobi

It was all for charity so everyone was happy to agree to do it.

I got the short straw by going first and always knew I would have to run the gauntlet of the other lads who were watching.

There was a lot of banter with the all the lads shouting and screaming but it was good fun and all for a great cause.

Matt Jarvis

The name's Stearman...

...Richard Stearman

I didn't have any nerves.

I work very hard on getting a good body and if you've got it you should be proud to show it off!

It's also for such a great cause and is something we were all very keen to do.

George Elokobi

Applause from all for a job well done

I enjoyed it and thought it was a nice show! It wasn't easy because it was my first time doing something like this but I learned a lot! It's nice to do something like this away from football – I think we should all be ready to open our minds from time to time.

Adlene Guedioura

A different sort of kitbag for Adlene Guedioura

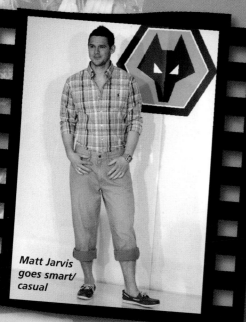

Matt Jarvis goes smart/ casual

Those of us who weren't modelling were naturally very keen to come along and the support the lads.

We were rooting for them all to do a good job – of course we were!

To be fair they all looked good out there.

I was sat with Jonah and we don't need hairdressers and all that to have our own little fashion show, although the truth is that we bottled it and didn't make the cut!

Karl Henry

29

WHO SAID IT? QUOTES QUIZ

The 10 quotes below were all said by an official or player at Wolves during the 2009/10 season.

Can you match the quote to the person concerned? Answers on Page 61.

Pick the speaker from the following list:

Ronald Zubar; Karl Henry; Mick McCarthy; Sylvan Ebanks-Blake; Jody Craddock; Marcus Hahnemann; Steve Morgan; Jez Moxey; Kevin Doyle; Matt Murray

1 "Just playing games is massive for me. Before the start of the season I always thought I was just going to be on the sidelines being back-up. That hasn't been the case so far. Day in, day out training it does get a little harder for me, but I try to keep my standards high and hopefully it will pay off on the pitch which is where it counts. And when I'm on that pitch I feel as young as the next man. "

2 "It's not like going into Tescos and picking a can of beans off the shelf. It's always a difficult time with all the negotiations involved. "

3 "I used to watch Manchester United as a kid and loved to see Eric Cantona play. Some of the goals he scored were incredible and I loved his attitude. I think some people thought he was arrogant but that was fine with me – he was a great player and I think everyone respected his abilities. "

4 "It's a beautiful result! My wife Amanda is away so my brother-in-law came to the game along with my buddies Justin and Shelee. Justin plays bass for Tool which is my favourite band. My wife was stressing about missing the game because it becomes part of the ritual and superstition if you like but everything worked out ok. "

5 "As ever we appreciate the excellent support of our fans who follow the team in such large numbers up and down the country and hope they realise that every decision made by the manager is one which has the best interests of the club at heart. We win some games and we lose others but at the end of the season we all hope that we will still be in the Premier League and will be able to celebrate that landmark together. "

6 "The fans have been brilliant and that touches me. I've done nothing this year to give them a reason to sing my name and chant but they've done it. I do take all that on board and am touched by it and I have a lot of respect for them for that. "

7 "The lads played Manchester City earlier in the season and Emmanuel Adebayor scored the only goal of the game. There was some talk a few days later of how he'd really shown a good turn of pace to get away from one of our defenders with the lads saying they hadn't really realised how quick he was. 'He's not that quick'," said Andy Keogh. He's the same speed as me, he's just got longer legs so he gets there quicker! "

8 "Straightaway he said to me: 'I want to sign you, we're paying a lot of money for you but if you're not doing well you won't play.' No nicey nicey, messing about. We had a great conversation, a good chat and that was it. He was straight to the point. "

9 "Jack Bauer is just a joke. He never makes a wrong decision. He can fly planes, he can fly helicopters, and de-fuse bombs. He's got an immune system that means whatever he is exposed to he survives. He can perform transplants. He's got everything in his locker and if he was a footballer I think he'd be the top footballer there is. "

10 "I received a lovely letter which read: 'Thank you for taking the pressure off me. I've really had a tough time of late, all the best, Tiger'. I've heard he's driving around Florida in an open-top car singing my name. I've had another from Thierry Henry as well. He seems to think I've taken some of the heat off him as well. "

YOUNG WOLVES

The Young Wolves club has always proved extremely popular at Molineux, offering supporters under the age of 17 the chance to become part of the pack and enjoy a host of benefits.

And membership for the current season is well and truly open!

For the annual membership fee of £15, supporters immediately receive two exclusive joining gifts, a personalised membership card, entry to Wolves Loyalty Scheme and the allocation of 50 loyalty points.

Then there's entry to two designated Barclays Premier League home games at Molineux – ABSOLUTELY FREE – not to mention discounts off Wolves Soccer Schools and at the club's official retail stores (subject to terms and conditions).

There's also an exclusive Christmas card and two e-newsletters per season packed with a host of news stories and competitions.

On top of all this comes the opportunity to attend special events, including the pre-season photocall and the always-popular Christmas Parties with the players, as well as entry into draws to be an away mascot or for tickets for away games via the 'Junior Ticket Exchange' scheme.

Pictured here are some of the activities enjoyed by Young Wolves over the last year – to find out more or to become part of the club call **0871 222 1877** or visit **www.wolves.co.uk**

Young Wolves is just one of the many initiatives at Wolves designed to attract the next generation of supporters to Molineux, with the award-winning Wolves 4 Family Football scheme now into its third successful year.

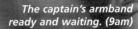

A MATCHDAY
IN THE LIFE...

Ever wondered what sort of activity goes on at Molineux on a matchday?

Apart from what happens in the 90 minutes on the pitch of course!

Moving the goalposts – up they go! (7am)

Shirts all laid out and ready to go. (9am)

A stadium tour before the game. (11.45am)

It's fair to say the stadium is a hive of activity from early on the morning of a matchday to a few hours after full-time catering for fans, corporate customers and the media as well as ensuring the stadium is in tip-top condition with all the necessary safety procedures followed.

Here below is a snapshot of some of the off-field routines which are usually adhered to, based on the traditional kick-off time of 3pm on a Saturday.

7am: Groundstaff arrive. Pitch is mowed either once or more often depending on circumstances. During the morning, pitch is marked out, goalposts erected and other signage put out and the surface then watered.

8am: Stadium safety officials, maintenance and cleaning staff arrive at Molineux to begin checks of facilities and equipment and to deal with any problems. Stadium tests including PA system and floodlight checks carried out before the day of the game. Kit usually placed in home dressing room the night before game with dressing rooms all checked and prepared.

9am: Ticket Office and Family Information Centre opens. PA announcer prepares matchday music mix on playout computer and edits any specific music tracks required for singers or presentations. All PA systems prepared and checked in corporate areas.

10am: Fitness and medical staff arrive at Molineux to ensure everything present and correct and ready for team later.

11am: Host broadcasters (currently Sky or BBC) carry out tests of their cameras and equipment. Huge broadcast trucks already on site from Friday evening. Ticket Collection kiosks open for collections.

11.30am: Management and first team squad arrive at hotel for pre-match meal. Various match sponsors arrive at Molineux.

11.45am: Sponsors are taken on full tour of stadium.

12pm: Senior stewarding staff arrive. Press start to arrive and head for media suite for refreshments. Any final rehearsals for singers or dancers performing as part of matchday entertainment.

12.15pm: Senior stewarding staff briefing.

The referees' room awaits the officials. (12.30pm)

12.30pm: Officials arrive at Molineux to begin their preparations.

1pm: Players start to arrive at Molineux from hotel. Stewards briefing. Corporate guests arrive. Matchday programmes on sale around the ground.

1.15pm: Stewards carry out a 'sweep' of the stadium including safety checks.

1.25pm: Safety announcement over PA system to ensure all staff and visiting stewards are aware of matchday procedures.

1.30pm: Turnstiles open. Corporate guests enjoy pre-match meals. Visiting team coach arrives. Matchday mascot arrives.

Visiting team – in this case Manchester United – arrive. (1.30pm)

1.45pm: Interview with Wolves player not involved in game in all corporate areas.

2pm: Managers and captains meet to swop team-sheets and pass on to officials.

2.10pm: Teams announced to corporate guests and media.

2.15pm: Players warm up on the pitch. Another first-team player not involved visits Paycare Disabled Lounge to meet supporters.

2.30pm: PA announcer officially welcomes everyone to the stadium and reads teams, birthdays and any items of club news before playing a track from a featured local band.

2.50pm: Referee rings bell in dressing room for first time to alert players.

2.52pm: Referee rings bell again as final alert and his assistants knock on dressing room doors.

The players emerge from the tunnel (2.54pm)

The pre-match photograph with mascots. (2.54pm)

2.54pm: Teams emerge from tunnel. Teams are read out again as players shake hands and then captains meet officials in centre circle. Captains toss coin with mascots watched by main match sponsors.

3pm: Kick off! CCTV cameras in constant operation to monitor crowd as they are from 9am until 6pm on matchdays. Cleaning and maintenance staff usually kept busy throughout the 90 minutes. Ticket Office staff work out attendance to be announced before full-time.

3.45: Half-time. Media and corporate guests head to suites for refreshments. Half-time entertainment and presentations. Ground staff work on divoting and pitch repair work.

4.50pm: Full-time. Supporters reminded via PA system of next game and any important club news. Ticket Office re-opens.

5pm: Wolves man of the match is taken to main match sponsors for presentation. Stewards carry out post match 'sweep' of stadium and make safety checks.

Interview with man of the match (5pm)

5.15pm: Managers of both teams and selected players carry out interviews for press. DVD's provided to home and away managers and officials and Wolves chairman Steve Morgan.

5.30pm: Managers meet in office for post-match drink. Stewards stand down.

6pm-6.30pm: Opposition coach leaves. Stadium staff stand down and corporate guests and media depart. Catering staff clear hospitality areas and ensure turnaround for any evening events. Broadcasting trucks complete de-rigging of equipment and leave between 6pm and 7pm.

PLAYER PROFILES

MATT MURRAY

POSITION: Goalkeeper
BORN: Solihull, 02/05/81
FORMER CLUBS: Slough, Kingstonian, Tranmere, Hereford (all loans)
JOINED WOLVES: May, 1998 (signed pro)
FASCINATING FACT: Made his England Under-21 debut against Slovakia in October, 2002, in a team also including Gareth Barry, Michael Carrick and Joe Cole.

JODY CRADDOCK

POSITION: Defender
BORN: Redditch, 25/07/75
FORMER CLUBS: Cambridge, Sunderland, Sheffield United (loan), Stoke (loan)
JOINED WOLVES: July, 2003
FASCINATING FACT: Was the only Wolves player to find the net in November, 2009, a spell when he scored four consecutive Wolves goals.

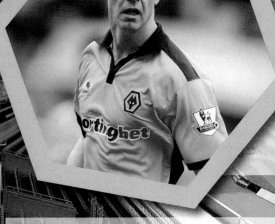

CARL IKEME

POSITION: Goalkeeper
BORN: Birmingham, 08/06/86
FORMER CLUBS: Accrington Stanley, Stockport, Charlton, Sheffield United, QPR (all loans)
JOINED WOLVES: July, 2003 (signed pro)
FASCINATING FACT: First three starts for Wolves were all in the Carling Cup, and two of them (Chesterfield and Rotherham) ended in penalty shootouts.

KARL HENRY

POSITION: Midfielder
BORN: Wolverhampton, 26/11/82
FORMER CLUBS: Stoke, Cheltenham (loan)
JOINED WOLVES: July, 2006
FASCINATING FACT: A boyhood Wolves fan, Karl's first Molineux appearance on trial in a pre-season friendly against Aston Villa was also Steve Bull's last competitive outing at the stadium as he played the opening few minutes of his 20th anniversary game.

WAYNE HENNESSEY

POSITION: Goalkeeper
BORN: Anglesey, 24/01/87
FORMER CLUBS: Stockport (loan)
JOINED WOLVES: April, 2005 (signed pro)
FASCINATING FACT: Set a record with Stockport by keeping clean sheets in his first nine senior appearances, in which Stockport won every game.

STEPHEN WARD

POSITION: Left Back/Midfielder.
BORN: Dublin, 20/08/85.
FORMER CLUBS: Bohemians.
JOINED WOLVES: January, 2007.
FASCINATING FACT: When joining Wolves, the striker-turned-defender moved for a record fee for the Eircom League of Ireland at the time.

MICHAEL KIGHTLY

POSITION: Winger

BORN: Basildon, 24/01/86

FORMER CLUBS: Southend, Farnborough (loan), Grays Athletic

JOINED WOLVES: November, 2006

FASCINATING FACT: Six months before joining Wolves, Kightly was picking up the Man of the Match award in the FA Trophy Final as Grays beat Woking at Upton Park.

MATT JARVIS

POSITION: Winger

BORN: Middlesbrough, 22/05/86

FORMER CLUBS: Millwall, Gillingham

JOINED WOLVES: June, 2007

FASCINATING FACT: Son of Linda and Nick who were both British Number One Table Tennis Players, Jarvis's first ever goal for Gillingham was a winning goal – against Wolves!

KEVIN FOLEY

POSITION: Defender/Midfielder

BORN: Luton, 01/11/84

FORMER CLUBS: Luton

JOINED WOLVES: August, 2007

FASCINATING FACT: Missed just one league game of Wolves' Championship-winning 2008/09 season, earning the Supporters' Player of the Year award in the process.

DAVE EDWARDS

POSITION: Midfielder
BORN: Shrewsbury, 03/02/86
FORMER CLUBS: Shrewsbury, Luton
JOINED WOLVES: January, 2008
FASCINATING FACT: Enjoyed contrasting Shrewsbury and Wolves debuts, both against Scunthorpe, seeing the Shrews relegated in the former and scoring in a 2-0 win in the latter.

SYLVAN EBANKS-BLAKE

POSITION: Striker
BORN: Cambridge, 29/03/86
FORMER CLUBS: Manchester United, Royal Antwerp (loan), Plymouth
JOINED WOLVES: January, 2008
FASCINATING FACT: Sylvan, Championship Golden Boot winner for two successive seasons, was actually named after a racehorse.

GEORGE ELOKOBI

POSITION: Left Back
BORN: Cameroon, 31/01/86
FORMER CLUBS: Colchester, Chester (loan)
JOINED WOLVES: January, 1986
FASCINATING FACT: Moved to England from Cameroon at the age of 15 and combined studying at college with playing non-league for Dulwich Hamlets.

SAM VOKES

POSITION: Striker

BORN: Southampton, 21/10/89

FORMER CLUBS: Bournemouth, Leeds (loan)

JOINED WOLVES: May, 2008

FASCINATING FACT: Scored within 36 seconds of his Wales-under-21 debut against Northern Ireland and within a minute on his first Wolves appearance after coming off the bench at Plymouth.

RICHARD STEARMAN

POSITION: Defender

BORN: Wolverhampton, 19/08/87

FORMER CLUBS: Leicester

JOINED WOLVES: June, 2008

FASCINATING FACT: Born in Wolverhampton and spent the first five years of his life in the city before moving to Leicester, returning 16 years later when signing for Wolves.

DAVID JONES

POSITION: Midfielder

BORN: Southport, 04/11/84

FORMER CLUBS: Manchester United, Preston (loan), NEC Nijmegen (loan), Derby

JOINED WOLVES: June, 2008

FASCINATING FACT: Captained Manchester United to success in the 2003 FA Youth Cup, playing alongside Wolves team-mate Sylvan Ebanks-Blake.

CHRISTOPHE BERRA

POSITION: Defender
BORN: Edinburgh, 31/01/85
FORMER CLUBS: Heart of Midlothian
JOINED WOLVES: January, 2009
FASCINATING FACT: Succeeded Craig Gordon to become Hearts captain at the age of 22, then the youngest skipper in the Scottish Premier League.

MARCUS HAHNEMANN

POSITION: Goalkeeper
BORN: Seattle, 15/06/72
FORMER CLUBS: Seattle Sounders, Colorado Rapids, Fulham, Rochdale (loan), Reading
JOINED WOLVES: June, 2009
FASCINATING FACT: Is the holder of the 'record' of longest time elapsed between international caps for the USA, appearing in 2003 for the first time since his previous appearance in 1994.

NENAD MILIJAŠ

POSITION: Midfielder
BORN: Serbia, 30/04/83
FORMER CLUBS: FK Zemun, Red Star Belgrade
JOINED WOLVES: June, 2009
FASCINATING FACT: First goal in English football for Wolves against Bolton in December, 2009, went on to be voted Wolves' Goal of the Season.

KEVIN DOYLE

POSITION: Striker
BORN: Adamstown, 18/09/83
FORMER CLUBS: Cork City, Reading
JOINED WOLVES: June, 2009
FASCINATING FACT: Worked in his parents' pub as a youngster and also mucked out stables for his father who breeds racehorses.

RONALD ZUBAR

POSITION: Defender
BORN: Guadeloupe, 20/09/85
FORMER CLUBS: Caen, Marseille
JOINED WOLVES: July, 2009
FASCINATING FACT: Counts Didier Drogba and William Gallas among his footballing mates and has a younger brother Stephane who is also a professional.

GEOFFREY MUJANGI BIA (on season long loan)

POSITION: Winger.
BORN: DR Congo, 12/08/89.
FORMER CLUBS: Charleroi.
JOINED WOLVES: January, 2010.
FASCINATING FACT: Moved to Belgium as a child, and made his senior international debut against Chile in May, 2009.

ADLENE GUEDIOURA

POSITION: Midfielder
BORN: France, 12/11/85
FORMER CLUBS: RSC Charleroi
JOINED WOLVES: January, 2010
FASCINATING FACT: Followed in the footsteps of father Nacer by becoming an Algerian international while his mother was a Spanish basketball player.

JELLE VAN DAMME

POSITION: Defender
BORN: Lokeren, 10/10/83
FORMER CLUBS: Ajax, Southampton, Werder Bremen (loan), Anderlecht
JOINED WOLVES: June, 2010
FASCINATING FACT: Wife Elke used to be a professional tennis player on the women's circuit, and she is sister to Grand Slam Champion Kim Clijsters.

STEVEN FLETCHER

POSITION: Striker
BORN: Shrewsbury, 26/03/87
FORMER CLUBS: Hibernian, Burnley
JOINED WOLVES: June, 2010
FASCINATING FACT: Played for Hibernian against Barcelona in a friendly at Murrayfield which was watched by the entire Wolves squad during their pre-season tour of Scotland in 2008.

STEVEN MOUYOKOLO

POSITION: Defender
BORN: France, 24/01/87
FORMER CLUBS: Gueugnon, Boulogne, Hull
JOINED WOLVES: June, 2010
FASCINATING FACT: Before joining Hull, Steven helped Boulogne achieve promotion to French Ligue One for the first time in their history

STEPHEN HUNT

POSITION: Winger
BORN: Portlaoise, 01/08/81
FORMER CLUBS: Crystal Palace, Brentford, Reading, Hull
JOINED WOLVES: June, 2010
FASCINATING FACT: As well as football, Stephen was a talented hurler in his formative years representing Waterford at Under-15 and Under-16 levels

ANDY KEOGH

POSITION: Striker
BORN: Dublin, 16/05/86
FORMER CLUBS: Leeds, Scunthorpe, Bury (loan)
JOINED WOLVES: January, 2007
FASCINATING FACT: Secured Wolves' first ever away win in the Barclays Premier League by heading home the winner against Wigan in August, 2009

GREG HALFORD

POSITION: Midfielder
BORN: Chelmsford, 08/12/84
FORMER CLUBS: Colchester, Reading, Sunderland, Charlton (loan), Sheffield United (loan)
JOINED WOLVES: July, 2009
FASCINATING FACT: Appeared for England's Under-20 side at the Toulon tournament in 2005, making his debut against Portugal, and scoring his first goal in a win against South Korea two days later

THE YOUNG ONES

DANNY BATH

POSITION: Defender

BORN: Brierley Hill, 21/09/90

SAM WINNALL

POSITION: Striker

BORN: Wolverhampton, 19/01/91

DAVID DAVIS

POSITION: Midfielder

BORN: Smethwick, 20/02/91

NATHANIEL MENDEZ-LAING

POSITION: Winger/Striker

BORN: Birmingham, 15/04/92

JOHNNY DUNLEAVY

POSITION: Defender

BORN: Donegal, 03/07/91

JAMIE RECKORD

POSITION: Defender

BORN: Wolverhampton, 09/03/92

ASHLEY HEMMINGS

POSITION: Striker

BORN: Lewisham, 03/03/91

NATHAN ROONEY

POSITION: Midfielder

BORN: Shrewsbury, 02/10/91

SCOTT MALONE

POSITION: Defender

BORN: Rowley Regis, 25/03/91

AARON MCCAREY

POSITION: Goalkeeper

BORN: County Monaghan, 14/01/92

43

WOLVES ACADEMY
THE NEXT GENERATION

words by Academy Manager Kevin Thelwell

Enjoy it: Jack Price

 What does it take to be a success at the Wolves Academy? Here Academy manager Kevin Thelwell pinpoints some key factors along with highlighting the efforts of players who have shown those qualities.

HARD WORK

It is becoming harder every year for young players at all Premier League clubs to make the step up to the first team. The Premier League is seen as being the best in the world and that is due to the fact that the very best players play in it! Young players must work as hard as they can on their game to ensure they are the very best they can be to get a chance to break through. One of our hardest working players is young James Spray who has already been involved in a Premier League squad at just 17 years of age. James works very hard at his game and we hope this will pay off for him in the seasons to come.

TECHNIQUE

All of our young players must work hard to develop excellent technique if they are to play for our first team. This is becoming more and more important especially as the Premier League is so quick. Players must be able to handle the ball under pressure if they are to be successful. First-year scholar Anthony Forde is a great example of this. When he first joined us we had difficulty in figuring out which was his strongest foot as he was so good with both. Once again, Anthony spends a huge amount of time practising his techniques and skills to allow him to get to this level.

ATTITUDE

Having the right attitude is vitally important to us at Wolves. Players must be polite, courteous and respectful both on and off the field of play. They must work hard to become footballers but just as hard to become good people as well. Kristian Kostrna is a fine example of this. Kristian is from Slovakia and left his home and family to join us this summer. At 16 years of age he has learnt fluent English and is already developing into an excellent example for our young schoolboy players. Kristian is currently a Slovakian International at Under-17 and Under-19 level and has already played for our Youth team.

BE PREPARED TO LISTEN

As a young player there is much to learn and it is important that you take on board all of the advice that will help you with your game from your coaches. Small improvements can make a big difference when they are added together and you should use guidance from coaches to take your game to the next level. Nathan Rooney worked hard last season as the Captain of the youth team to listen and learn from the people around him and that culminated in him also captaining the reserve team and earning his first professional contract. Nathan was also named Academy Player of the Year.

MAKE EVERY DAY YOUR MASTERPIECE

As young footballers it is important to recognise that you must try to be at your best for every training session and every game. By consistently setting such high standards players get into the habit of performing at their very best. Young Johnny Gorman is one of the best trainers in the Academy, also giving his all and working hard to improve his game. This hard work is starting to pay off as, at just 17 years of age, he has already been capped at senior level for Northern Ireland.

BELIEVE IN YOURSELF!

We often say to our young players that the only thing that can stop them reaching their goals is themselves. It is important that players believe in themselves and are confident in their own abilities. Somebody has to play for our first team why can't it be you? Young striker Liam McAlinden is a real example of this and always has a really positive and confident nature. He is fast developing into a great striker and has already scored goals for the youth team, reserves and his national team Northern Ireland (Even though he was born in Cannock!)

PRACTICE, PRACTICE, PRACTICE!

The only way that you will improve is if you practice as much as you possibly can. Experts are currently suggesting that to become a top class footballer it will take at least 10,000 hours of practice to get to the required level – so get kicking that ball around! One of our young players Zeli Ismail is a real example of this. Zel loves to play and sometimes it is difficult to get him and others off the training ground – he would stay out there all day if he could! And even when he gets home he is out with the ball and his mates!

ENJOY IT!

The reason that you play football as young children is because you enjoy it, this should never be forgotten. If you don't enjoy it, then this will show in your performances! One of our young players Jack Price is a real example of this. Jack loves to play and always has a smile on his face. He is always bright and bubbly around the training ground and this makes a difference to his team mates and the staff.

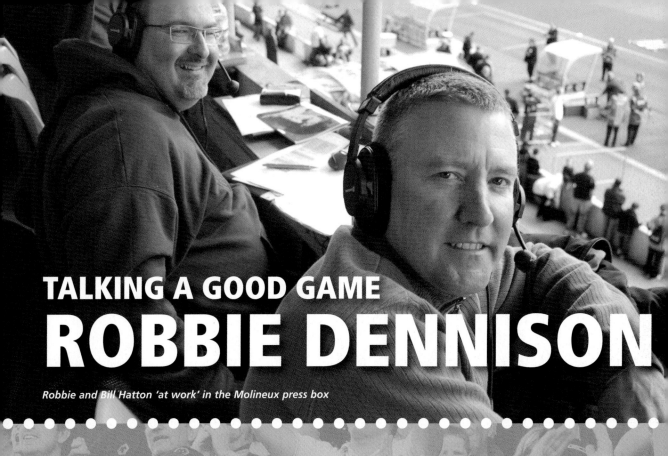

TALKING A GOOD GAME
ROBBIE DENNISON

Robbie and Bill Hatton 'at work' in the Molineux press box

Former Wolves favourite Robbie Dennison was well known for his tricks and wing wizardry when gracing the flanks of Molineux during his time as a player.

But there are no sidesteps for the genial Irishman in his current footballing vocation as a co-commentator on Wolves games for Beacon Radio.

Dennison, who made over 350 appearances and scored 49 goals for Wolves between 1987 and 1997, has become well-known in recent years for his articulate and knowledgeable summarising alongside Bill Hatton.

And yet he admits it wasn't an area he thought about going into while he was still a player.

"I never had a problem with being interviewed as a player but at the same time I didn't think about being on the other side of the microphone," says Dennison.

"Towards the end of my career I started doing my coaching badges but that didn't really work out for me and I ended up stopping.

"I'd bumped into Bill a few times during my testimonial year and at other events and one day he asked me to do a game on the Wolf radio station – and it all took off from there.

"I have to say it did take a bit of getting used to but gradually I got into it and felt comfortable.

"It's just talking about the game really, which I've always enjoyed doing, and I've learned a great deal from my time as a player.

"Having said that, I probably couldn't do something like interviewing the manager after a game which would be a different matter entirely – I'll leave that one to the others!"

Regular listeners to the commentaries on Beacon will know that Dennison and his partner-in-crime Hatton do tend to get slightly excited from time to time.

The famous last gasp victory over Charlton at the Valley during Wolves' Championship winning season is a prime example.

But the ex-Northern Ireland international believes that's par for the course given the nature of the job.

"For me, it helps that it's Wolves," he says.

"It's a club that played such a big part in my career and I want to see them do well.

"If I wasn't doing the radio work I'd be up there in the stands watching the games myself.

"We're doing the commentaries for the Wolves fans so I think people want a bit of bias in there because we want the club to win games and that's why the passion comes out."

From Hatton's point of view, he remains delighted to be continuing his working association with Dennison which has now spanned many years.

"Robbie offers a unique insight that only an ex-professional and indeed a former Wolves star can do," he says.

"He has great expertise, is very articulate and puts his views across in a way that connects with the listeners.

"We've also had some good laughs along the way, and hopefully it works well in partnership with my commentary style.

"Robbie is also always approachable and has a great sense of humour – I think everyone who has met him knows he's certainly no 'Billy Big Time'.

"But even with all that he's never afraid to tell it how it is and pull no punches during the commentary which is exactly what you need."

Dennison, who combines covering matches home and away with other business interests, enjoyed plenty of success at Molineux as a player, helping the club to back-to-back promotions from the lower divisions and scoring spectacular Wembley goals in the Sherpa Van Trophy win and Football League Centenary tournament.

His hopes of a goal in one of his 18 international caps were once denied by a certain Mick McCarthy, who cleared a Dennison effort off the line during a 3-0 win for the Republic in Dublin.

The Wolves boss has been forgiven!

"Mick has done a great job to take Wolves where they are from the time he came in as manager," says Dennison.

"And I think with the stadium plans as well, these are exciting times for the club.

"The Chairman is clearly very ambitious and the club is being run well financially and hopefully they will now be able to push on."

And when they do, Dennison, complete with headphones, will be watching eagerly from the sidelines.

Top: Celebrating with Andy Mutch after the Sherpa Van Trophy final.
Middle: More celebrations after Wolves won the Third Division championship.
Bottom: Trying to make tracks against former club West Bromwich Albion.

47

A QUESTION OF WOLVES HISTORY

Have a go at the questions below relating to events of Wolves past and discover if you really are the Mind of Molineux!

1. Which Wolves legend wrote his name into history by becoming the first England substitute when replacing Jackie Milburn against Belgium in 1950?

2. Which two brothers found the net in an entertaining five-goal clash between Wolves and Hull in February, 2006?

3. Which two players hold the record for Wolves of making 18 appearances for the club in European competition fixtures?

4. What record was broken at Molineux on the first day of the 2000/01 season as Wolves met Sheffield Wednesday?

5. Which player scored twice at Reading in 1985 to secure Wolves a draw and bring an end to the Royals record-breaking run of 13 successive wins at the start of the season?

6. Reverend Kenneth Hunt achieved which unique feat when a Wolves player in 1908?

7. Wolves were the first team ever to reach 7,000 league goals, a feat they achieved in December, 2005. But who got the goal?

8. Wolves hold the joint record for the best away win in the top flight thanks to a 9-1 success in 1955. Who was it against?

9. Wolves had only ever fielded two players whose surname began with the letter 'I' up until the start of the 21st century. But that soon became five thanks to three players who turned out for the club during the 2002/03 campaign. Who were they?

10. What did Peter Knowles receive from Portsmouth after scoring one of the goals in a 3-2 win at Fratton Park enroute to Wolves' promotion in 1967?

ANSWERS ON PAGE 61

KEVIN DOYLE

WHAT IF NOT...
A FOOTBALLER?

Trying to become a footballer is a dream of most youngsters with any sort of interest in the game, and of course the Wolves players are no different.

But what would the current squad have ended up doing if they hadn't quite made it in football? Or what other career would they have wanted to pursue? The Wolves Annual caught up with the lads to find out more…

DAVID JONES

Tennis Player: I wasn't bad at tennis as a youngster and once played Alex Bogdanovic at the Solihull International tournament. I didn't beat him, but I should have done!

STEPHEN WARD

Policeman: My Dad's a Policeman over in Ireland and you often want to follow what your Dad does. I think I'd have been quite good!

MICHAEL KIGHTLY

PE Teacher: I was actually part-way through the training at college before I became a footballer.

GEOFFREY MUJANGI BIA

Football Agent!

MATT JARVIS

Something else in Sport: I used to do everything when I was a kid so I think it would have been a different sport.

STEPHEN HUNT

Golfer: I'm not any good, but I could have taken travelling the world to play golf.

KARL HENRY

City Trader in London: I reckon that's definitely something I could have carried off!

JODY CRADDOCK

PE Teacher: Everyone probably thinks I'd have been an artist but I wasn't that good at art at the time.

RICHARD STEARMAN

Attend University: It would have involved something to do with sport, maybe Sports Science perhaps.

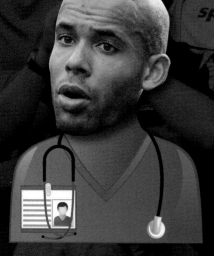

MATT MURRAY

Vet or a Schoolteacher: They say never work with children or animals but I'd have been happy working with both. I'm not sure I'd have been clever enough for both mind you!

KEVIN DOYLE

Barman or Stable Boy: I used to work in a pub as a kid as well as helping out with my Dad's stables as he breeds racehorses. I'd probably have ended up doing either of those!

RONALD ZUBAR

Tennis Player: Or away from sport I'd have liked to have become a Doctor, as difficult as that would have been.

WAYNE HENNESSEY

Basketball Player: When I was young I played a bit of basketball which I enjoyed. I'd have liked a career in sport so I'd have tried for basketball if football hadn't happened.

DAVE EDWARDS

Attend University: I'm pretty confident the student life would have suited me perfectly!

SAM VOKES

Builder: Yep a builder – Id have gone for that.

GEORGE ELOKOBI

Attend University: I'm not sure what I'd have studied, but something would have come to me!

KEVIN FOLEY

Physiotherapist: I'd have wanted to do something involved in sport and I think being a physio would fit the bill.

STEVEN MOUYOKOLO

Doctor: I used to study Science and in particular biology and would have liked to have become a Doctor.

CHRISTOPHE BERRA

Fireman or a Policeman: Something like that would have appealed to me!

MICK MCCARTHY

And the gaffer? *Electrician:* I'd have been an electrician and probably gone down the mines. I wanted a trade and I was already in the process of trying to become an electrician. I never thought I'd get the gig as a footballer!

WORLD CUP WOLVES: PICTURE SPECIAL

The footballing summer was understandably dominated by the World Cup in South Africa – a tournament at which Wolves were heavily represented.

The selections of Marcus Hahnemann, Nenad Milijaš and Adlene Guedioura for their respective countries gave Wolves their highest representation at the tournament since Billy Wright, Eddie Clamp, Bill Slater and Peter Broadbent were picked for England in 1958.

Hahnemann didn't make it onto the pitch as the USA reached the last 16 by virtue of topping the group which also included England, but still enjoyed the big tournament experience as back-up to Tim Howard.

Milijaš made just one start as Serbia went out at the group stages, the midfielder playing for the first hour in their opening fixture against Ghana.

While Guedioura featured in all three Algeria games from the bench, including coming on for the final stages of the memorable draw with England.

Wolves boss Mick McCarthy meanwhile spent the first fortnight of the competition out in South Africa on co-commentary duties for the BBC while former Molineux defender Ricki Herbert enjoyed an impressive first managerial World Cup as New Zealand picked up three draws against opponents including 2006 winners Italy.

Elsewhere the new Burrda-sponsored Wolves shirt was given an airing by being shown to fans of all countries around the grounds while over 50 kits were donated to a special project for youngsters in a township near Johannesburg.

A new Wolves fan in the football team run by local Police Constable Olebogeng Ntaolang.

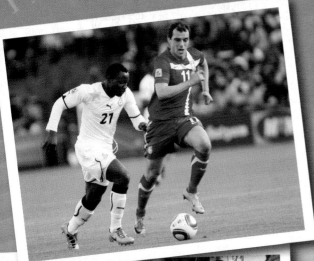

Top: The new Wolves shirt was taken out 'on tour' with fans at the World Cup and here a group of Ghana supporters are among those to get acquainted!

Middle: Wolves donated over 50 strips to boys from settlements in Hondeydew and Cosmo City in Johannesburg via the Nikos Haven Project in South Africa.

Bottom: Algeria's Adlene Guedioura came up against former West Bromwich Albion midfielder Robert Koren for Slovenia.

Top: Nenad Milijaš in action for Serbia chasing Ghana's Kwadwo Asamoah.

Middle: Mick with BBC commentator Steve Wilson at the Group B match between Greece and Argentina.

Bottom: Marcus Hahnemann consoles Marcus Edu after America's last 16 exit.

MATT JARVIS
A GOOD SPORT!

Given the fact that his parents Tony and Linda were both British number one Table Tennis players – it was always likely that Matt Jarvis would end up playing some form of sport.

And perhaps the only surprise is that Table Tennis was one of the few pastimes he didn't pursue too much as a sports-mad teenager.

"I didn't really play Table Tennis and never got pushed into it," recalls the winger.

"We had a table obviously but I'm sure Mum and Dad didn't want to come back home and play Table Tennis!

"I enjoyed it and still do socially as a fun game and when we went away on holiday there was always a table knocking about but that was about it."

Looking back, there probably wasn't enough time for Table Tennis!

"At school, I had something on every night," adds Jarvis.

"I was fairly good at a few different things as well as football such as swimming, cross country and athletics.

"I used to have stuff on every night of the week and some nights I was doing two – I became an expert at eating dinner in the car!

"But at the time, because I was just a kid and enjoying it, I never felt tired.

"Every morning I got up and felt fresh and wanted to do it all again!

"I enjoyed the training part of it although swimming was certainly the hardest.

"I'd be in the pool for two hours doing maybe 7.000 metres and while it wasn't boring it was hard work and you were using completely different muscles.

"I loved the competing aspect of swimming - it was just you on the blocks ready to go.

"In fact, I always wanted to win, whatever the sport, and still do!

"I'm sure all footballers are the same in terms of a competitive edge.

"Anything I do – even if it's maybe golf which I'm not very good at – I'll still want to try and be better than the other person."

Speaking of winning, despite all the different sports Jarvis pursued in his schooldays, when it came to a favourite there was only ever going to be one first choice.

"I always wanted to be a footballer and the other sports I liked more for the social side," he adds.

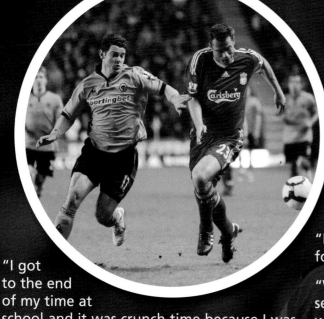

"I got to the end of my time at school and it was crunch time because I was never going to be able to fit everything in.

"And football was always going to be my first choice.

"As soon as you're trying to get a place on a YTS scheme you know you've got to concentrate on football.

"I was at Millwall for about six years through schoolboy level up until 16.

"They didn't offer me a YTS but on the same day I found out Gillingham got in touch and offered me something straightaway.

"I really enjoyed it at Gillingham – it's a fantastic club and the fans are great.

"Even as a YTS there were times when I travelled with the first team and I went away with them during pre-season.

"I made my debut for the first team at 17 against Sunderland when I came on as a substitute.

"And my first goal came against Wolves.

"That was a great day for us because we were on a really bad run before the match and we had a man sent off early on.

"I scored and then we hung on which was a great result and unfortunately Dave Jones lost his job.

"Then I moved here and it was the first thing that was brought up!"

It's been very much a positive story for Jarvis and Wolves since his arrival in 2007.

The wing wizard headed into the 2010/11 season with almost a century of appearances to his name and a fair few goals, and was particularly impressive as Wolves survived in the top flight for the first time in almost 30 years.

"Everyone's dream is to play in the Premier League and mine is exactly the same," he explains.

"If you can do that then you want to play for your country and I'm no different.

"When we first got into the league last season, for the first few weeks everyone was a bit like 'wow' – we're here lining up against all the big boys.

"But pretty quickly you realise you can't be phased by that and know that it's just 11 against 11.

"After that we enjoyed the challenge and came out of it really well.

"This season could well be even harder but we've got that experience now and know not to be afraid of anyone.

"The first priority is to survive and if that's achieved then it's about doing better than last season.

"With the squad we've got now then I think we are definitely capable of surviving again."

Ronald Zubar pictured visiting one of the Wolves' Soccer Schools, which take place at different venues during every school holiday.

WOLVES IN
THE COMMUNITY

Playing for Wolves is not just about heading to the Compton training ground every day or going out on the pitch to try and win a game at the weekend.

The club also take their position in the community of Wolverhampton and its surrounding area very seriously, and get involved in a host of different activities to boost support in the locality.

Wolves Community Trust is the club's official charitable trust including the Wolves Aid charity which since the arrival of chairman Steve Morgan has distributed thousands of pounds to local charities and community groups every year.

These activities are all boosted by a set of players who take their role in the community very seriously and support all the efforts of Wolves Community Trust.

These cover an extensive range of different events and campaigns, and now include initiatives incorporated by the Barclays Premier League.

Pictured are just a few examples of the players getting out and about in the community.

Above: Geoffrey Mujangi Bia about to get tackled at Woden!

Left: George Elokobi shares a joke as Wolves visited the Good Shepherd Soup Kitchen to hand out Christmas cheer.

Karl Henry and Chris Iwelumo try out for the Wolverhampton Rhinos Wheelchair Basketball team.

Above: Sylvan Ebanks-Blake makes a new young friend at the Walled Garden Project in Shifnal.

Left: Nenad Milijaš pictured going Back to School as Wolves' foreign contingent enjoyed some language lessons at Woden Primary School.

Below: Karl Henry gets to grips with some painting at the Beacon Centre for the Blind.

Kevin Doyle gets motoring during a festive visit to the Children's Ward at New Cross Hospital.

Marcus Hahnemann and Andrew Surman painting for the Prince's Trust at a project at Eastfields Community Centre.

57

FA CUP GLORY
50 YEARS ON

It was 50 years ago back in May that Wolves last lifted the famous FA Cup, courtesy of a 3-0 win against Blackburn on a sunny Wembley afternoon.

And the club marked that triumphant occasion from half a century ago by inviting the cup-winning heroes back to Molineux for the Barclays Premier League fixture with Blackburn in April.

So it was that victorious skipper Bill Slater, Ron Flowers, Malcolm Finlayson, George Showell and Gerry Harris received a rapturous welcome from a packed crowd at half-time of the match.

Not only that, but with Wolves having managed to secure loan of the FA Cup for the occasion, Slater was able to once again raise the trophy aloft, not at Wembley this time but Molineux instead.

The presence of two former Rovers players – ex-captain Ronnie Clayton and Bryan Douglas – added to the atmosphere as Wolves chairman Steve Morgan presented the trophy to the returning players.

Of the other Wolves heroes from that Blackburn triumph, Barry Stobart and Peter Broadbent were absent due to ill health while Des Horne now lives in South Africa.

The trio of players who have now passed on since the victory – Norman Deeley, Eddie Clamp and Jimmy Murray – were also remembered on the afternoon.

The 50-year anniversary prompted fans to recall their recollections of one of the many memorable days in Wolves' history, proving as it is the last time they have reached an FA Cup Final.

Top: Eddie Clamp and Bill Slater parade the trophy after Wolves' win.

Above: Norman Deeley is introduced to the Duke of Gloucester by captain Bill Slater.

Right: The returning heroes on the victorious bus ride through Wolverhampton.

It was also a season when they almost achieved the league double, having missed out on the league title by just a solitary point.

But they weren't to miss out at Wembley, a cross from Stobart seeing Mick McGrath put through his own net before two goals from Deeley secured the cup.

Now retired Express and Star Sports Editor and lifelong Wolves fan Steve Gordos was a young lad on that day, and went to the game at Wembley with his Dad.

Slater and Clayton with the cup, 50 years on.

o the present day... Malcolm Finlayson, George Showell, Bill Slater, Harris, Ronnie Clayton, Ron Flowers, Bryan Douglas were reunited presented with the cup by Wolves chairman Steve Morgan.

"I remember having to get up at a very early hour to get the steam-powered train to Wembley, one of the many specials laid on that day," recalls Steve.

"I remember walking towards the stadium and being impressed again by the twin towers, having been there a year earlier to see our own Billy Wright become the first man in the world to play in 100 internationals.

"Seeing the lush green turf sent a tingle down the spine.

"I had the feeling it would be our day - after all, we were the best team in the land.

"We had a brave goalkeeper in Malcolm Finlayson, reliable full backs in George Showell and Gerry Harris, superb England half backs Eddie Clamp, Bill Slater and Ron Flowers, ace goalscorers in Jimmy Murray and Norman Deeley, enthusiastic youngsters Des Horne and Barry Stobart and, of course, the maestro himself, Peter Broadbent."

Indeed it was Wolves day, also to the great delight of club historian Graham Hughes.

Living in Bristol at the time, Graham ended up sitting in the Blackburn end after one of his neighbours picked up tickets.

"I remember it was a boiling hot day as we sat amongst the Blackburn supporters, and it was all very good-natured with plenty of banter between us," he says.

"Both teams were original founder members of the Football League, which made the occasion even more special.

"It was a very proud moment for everyone from Wolves when Bill Slater and the team picked up the cup, and I remember the Blackburn captain Ronnie Clayton and the rest of the team going down the line and shaking the Wolves players' hands.

"And when we got back to Bristol Temple Meads station just after midnight, the porter spotted our Wolves rosettes and said 'well done'!"

Those two rosettes, along with a match programme and the whistle belonging to referee Kevin Howley on that day are now housed in trophy cabinets in Molineux reception, as pictured here with Graham.

Right: Wolves historian Graham Hughes pictured with a rosette, matchday programme and the referee's whistle from the final.

A GOLDEN FUTURE

If the FA Cup Final success of 1960 detailed on the previous pages forms part of Wolves' memorable past, then what of the future?

Wolves will be hoping things are looking bright on the pitch, but it certainly is off it as well, with developments in the infrastructure both at Molineux and the Compton training ground.

Over £1million was invested into improving the playing surfaces at the stadium and training ground during the summer, while plans were also unveiled for a new regeneration of Molineux costing in the region of £40million.

The plans are part of the exciting vision which chairman Steve Morgan had for the stadium when taking over the club in 2007, and could see the capacity extended to 36,000.

Above: What Molineux could look like over the next few years

QUIZ ANSWERS

WORDSEARCH (Page 24)

B	H	A	H	N	E	M	A	N	N
B	E	R	E	J	L	L	D	S	Z
C	N	R	N	L	O	T	O	D	U
K	R	J	R	F	K	N	L	O	B
I	Y	A	P	A	O	W	E	V	A
G	E	R	D	R	B	L	A	S	R
H	L	V	O	D	I	B	E	R	K
T	O	I	Y	G	O	A	T	Y	D
L	P	S	L	F	Z	C	R	O	T
Y	A	L	E	J	U	E	K	A	P

THE JUMBLED ELEVEN (Page 24)

THY CRAM KIM CC – **MICK MCCARTHY**

DINE LOVEY K – **KEVIN DOYLE**

LARK HE RYN – **KARL HENRY**

BRAN OR ZUALD – **RONALD ZUBAR**

CRY ROTER NON – **TERRY CONNOR**

LAKE BANK VANS BEYLS – **SYLVAN EBANKS-BLAKE**

SEW RAVE DADD – **DAVE EDWARDS**

HE YAWNS SEEN YEN – **WAYNE HENNESSEY**

DATE LONYY – **TONY DALEY**

IM A RATS TJV – **MATT JARVIS**

DOC DOC DAK JYR – **JODY CRADDOCK**

WHO SAID IT? (Page 30)

1. Jody Craddock
2. Steve Morgan
3. Ronald Zubar
4. Marcus Hahnemann
5. Jez Moxey
6. Sylvan Ebanks-Blake
7. Matt Murray
8. Kevin Doyle
9. Karl Henry
10. Mick McCarthy

A QUESTION OF WOLVES HISTORY (Page 48)

1. Jimmy Mullen.
2. Leon and Carl Cort.
3. Derek Dougan and John McAlle
4. Fastest sending off in England. Kevin Pressman after 13 seconds.
5. Derek Ryan.
6. Won an FA Cup winners' medal when Wolves beat Newcastle and then an Olympic gold in London when the United Kingdom beat Denmark in the final.
7. Seol Ki-Hyeon, against Crystal Palace.
8. Cardiff City.
9. Paul Ince, Denis Irwin and Ivar Ingimarsson.
10. The bill for a new ball! Knowles kicked one out of the ground in celebration